Cancer

First published in
United States in 1990 by
Franklin Watts
387 Park Avenue South
New York NY 10016

Design: David West
         Children's Book Design
Editor: Clare Llewellyn
Editorial Planning: Clark Robinson Ltd
Picture Research: Cecilia Weston-Baker
Illustrator: Ian Moores

Printed in Belgium

The publishers wish to acknowledge that the photographs
reproduced within this book have been posed by models or have
been obtained from photographic agencies.

Library of Congress Cataloging-in-Publication Data
Smail, Simon.
     Living with cancer / by Simon Smail.
        p.   cm. -- (Living with)
     Includes bibliographical references.
     Summary: Covers various aspects of life for children with cancer,
including their treatments and prospects for the future.
     ISBN 0-531-10859-7
     1. Tumors in children--Juvenile literature. [1.Cancer.]
I. Title. II. Series.
RC281.C4S6   1990
362.1'9892994--dc20   89-29464   CIP   AC

CONTENTS

Living with

Cancer

Dr Simon Smail

FRANKLIN WATTS
New York : London : Toronto : Sydney

WHAT IS CANCER?

The word cancer is a terrifying word for many people. Some people still believe that cancer is always a serious illness and that treatment will rarely bring about a cure. Yet the name "cancer" is used to describe not just one disease but a whole range of at least 200 different diseases. Many types of cancer are fairly easy to cure if they are treated early. More than one half of all cancers are now curable, although others are difficult to treat in their advanced stages.

All cancers have several things in common. First, a few cells in one area of the body start to grow in a disorganized way. These cells divide and multiply much too fast. This results in a collection of abnormal cells called a cancerous "tumor." Second, the abnormal cells sometimes spread into other tissues of the body – either into tissues that are near to the original tumor, or to those away from the original cancer site. Thirdly, the cells themselves have an abnormal structure.

Some tumors are called "benign" and are not cancerous. An ordinary wart, for example, is a benign tumor. It is only when the cells work abnormally that a tumor is cancerous. Many cancerous tumors may be started by a chemical or a virus, called a "carcinogen," which somehow interferes with the substances that control the cell – the DNA.

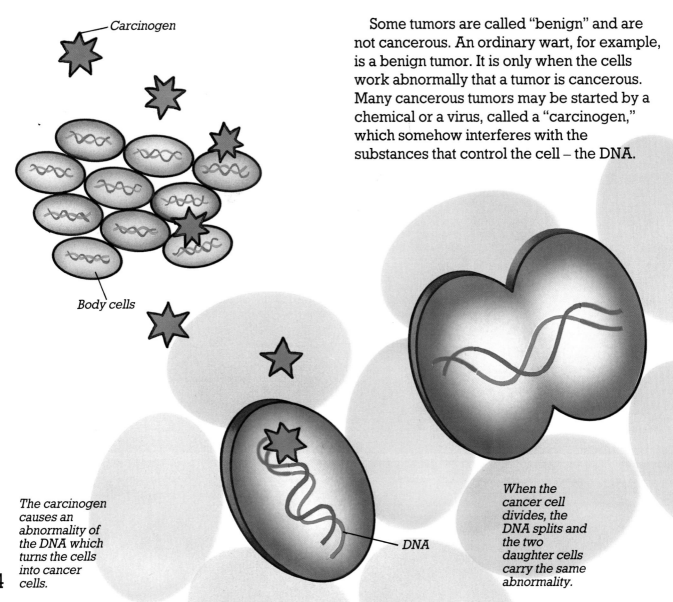

Carcinogen

Body cells

DNA

The carcinogen causes an abnormality of the DNA which turns the cells into cancer cells.

When the cancer cell divides, the DNA splits and the two daughter cells carry the same abnormality.

4

Local invasion

When cancer cells have produced a tumor, they continue to divide very quickly. The tumor will gradually grow larger and larger. Cancer cells may also start growing into nearby tissues, or can even spread into other parts of the body, crossing the natural divisions between one kind of tissue and another. For example, a cancer that starts in the lung can grow into the muscles or bones in the wall of the chest. This means that a tumor, if it is not treated, can become very large and could weigh several pounds.

Metastases

Sometimes, cancer cells grow into blood vessels. Once they are inside a blood vessel, cancer cells may break off and travel in the bloodstream to a different part of the body. A new cancerous tumor can then start to grow somewhere else. This is called "metastasis" ("metastases" is the plural). The same thing can happen if cancer cells grow into lymph vessels. Lymph vessels are a kind of drainage system for the body.

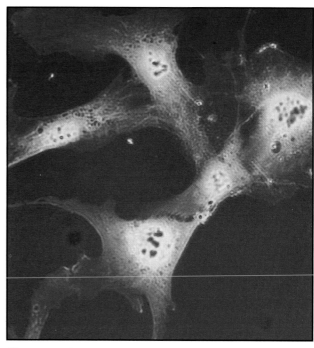

Cancerous tumor

Often cancer cells will break away and travel in the bloodstream to other parts of the body

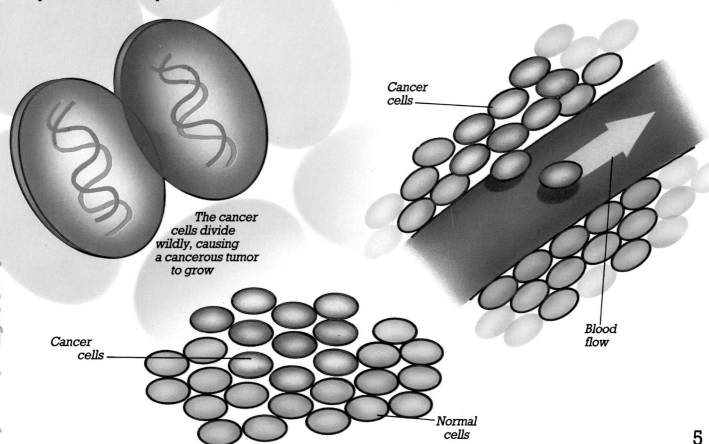

The cancer cells divide wildly, causing a cancerous tumor to grow

Cancer cells —

Cancer cells —

Normal cells

Blood flow

5

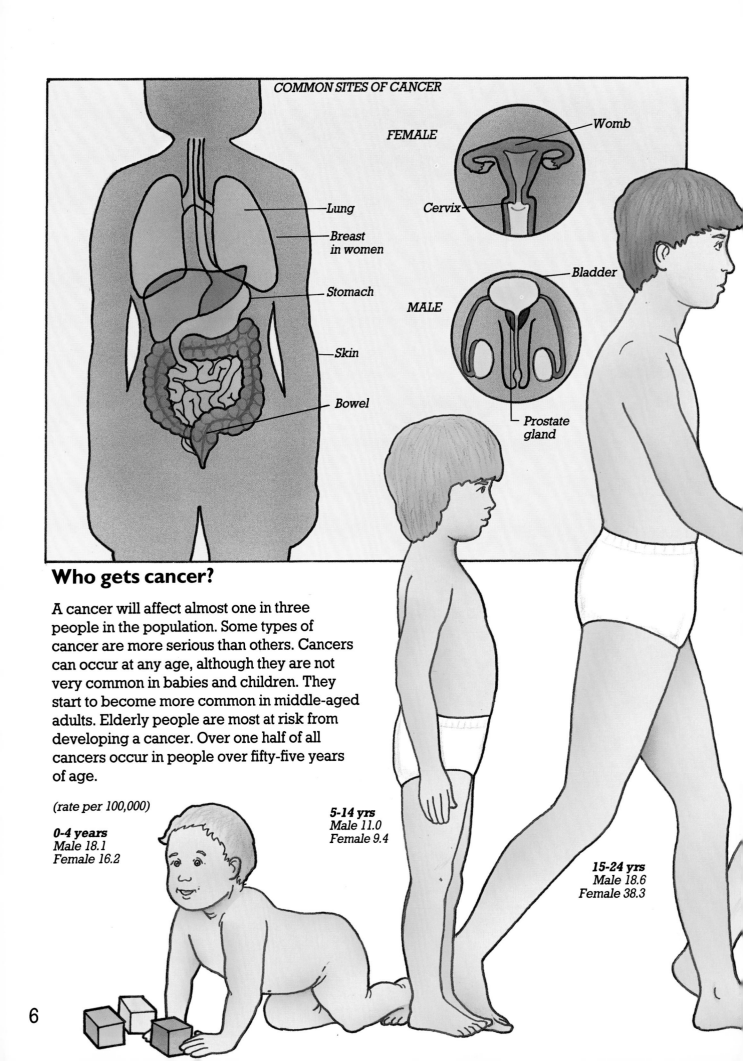

COMMON SITES OF CANCER

- Lung
- Breast in women
- Stomach
- Skin
- Bowel

FEMALE

- Womb
- Cervix

MALE

- Bladder
- Prostate gland

Who gets cancer?

A cancer will affect almost one in three people in the population. Some types of cancer are more serious than others. Cancers can occur at any age, although they are not very common in babies and children. They start to become more common in middle-aged adults. Elderly people are most at risk from developing a cancer. Over one half of all cancers occur in people over fifty-five years of age.

(rate per 100,000)

0-4 years
Male 18.1
Female 16.2

5-14 yrs
Male 11.0
Female 9.4

15-24 yrs
Male 18.6
Female 38.3

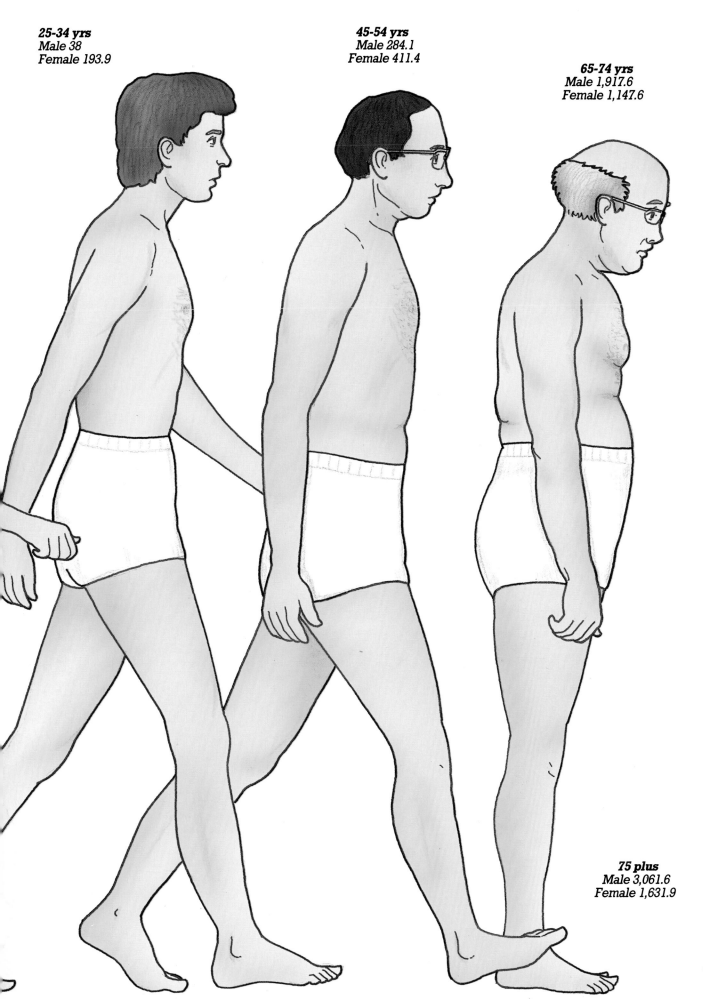

25-34 yrs
Male 38
Female 193.9

45-54 yrs
Male 284.1
Female 411.4

65-74 yrs
Male 1,917.6
Female 1,147.6

75 plus
Male 3,061.6
Female 1,631.9

7

WHAT CAUSES CANCERS?

Cancer is not one disease, but many. There are also many different causes of cancer. Sometimes it seems that certain types of cancer have a tendency to run in families. A few people may be born with a greater risk of developing a specific type of a cancer later in life. However, it is now thought that most cancers are caused by many different types of carcinogen. For example, the tars in cigarette smoke are now known to cause at least nine out of ten lung cancers. But carcinogens rarely cause a cancer as a result of just one exposure to the chemical. Repeated exposure over a long period of time is more likely. There may also be a long period of time between exposure to a carcinogen and the development of a cancer, perhaps ten years or more. There are carcinogens not only in cigarette smoke, but in some chemicals that people use at work and possibly in certain foods. Radiation, in the form of X rays or from radioactive material, may also act as a carcinogen.

THE CAUSES OF CANCER
(Percentage of all cancers)

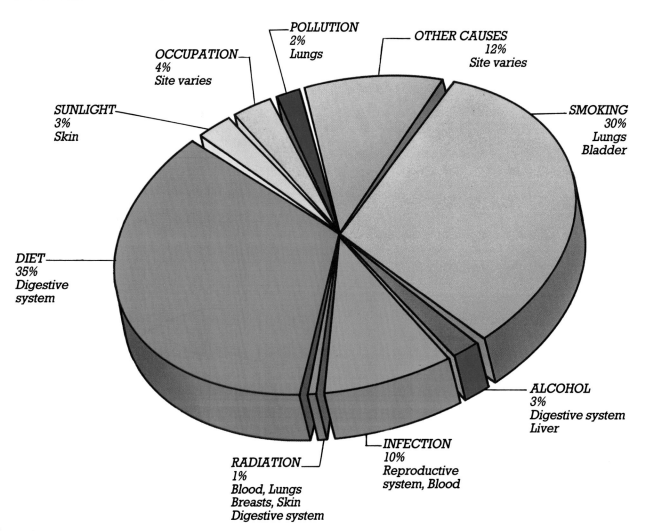

POLLUTION
2%
Lungs

OCCUPATION
4%
Site varies

OTHER CAUSES
12%
Site varies

SUNLIGHT
3%
Skin

SMOKING
30%
Lungs
Bladder

DIET
35%
Digestive
system

ALCOHOL
3%
Digestive system
Liver

RADIATION
1%
Blood, Lungs
Breasts, Skin
Digestive system

INFECTION
10%
Reproductive
system, Blood

The skin

Several different types of cancer can occur on the skin; the skin is also a very common place for completely benign tumors such as moles, and small growths called papillomas. One type of skin cancer most often develops in older people. Small cancerous growths appear on the face or the back of the hands. These form small lumps that slowly get bigger, may bleed a little and cause irritation. These cancerous tumors tend to grow very slowly, and hardly ever form metastases. Since they are easy to see, they are usually noticed early and treated.

Another form of cancer that starts in the skin is malignant melanoma. This is the result of a cancerous change in certain skin cells called "melanocytes." These cells carry a pigment called melanin, which darkens the skin when it is exposed to the sun. Often the cancer starts in a mole which gets bigger, becomes darker and may bleed. If the melanoma is not treated quickly, it may metastasize. There is now no doubt that too much exposure to the sun's rays can cause melanomas. Anyone who has been sunburned has a greater risk of developing melanomas in those parts of the body that have been burned.

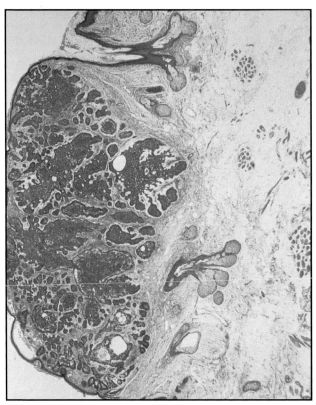

Skin cancer

Cancerous mole appears

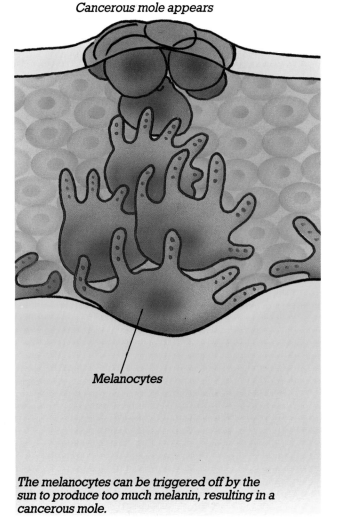

Melanocytes

The melanocytes can be triggered off by the sun to produce too much melanin, resulting in a cancerous mole.

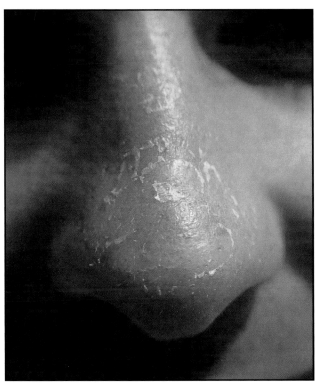

Sunburn

9

Blood and lymph cancers

Blood contains several different types of cells: red cells that carry oxygen around the body, and a number of different types of white cells. The white cells are called leukocytes. All the red cells and most of the white cells are made in bone marrow. This is a soft, fatty substance, which is found in many of the hollow bones of the body. Changes can take place in the bone marrow cells that normally produce the red and white blood cells, leading to the formation of abnormal bone marrow cells. These abnormal cells then circulate in the bloodstream, causing cancers which are all called leukemias. However, there are several different types of leukemia. Acute leukemias usually cause symptoms which appear suddenly and make the patient quite ill. Chronic leukemias cause fewer symptoms and are therefore more difficult to detect.

Some leukemias occur as a result of exposure to too much radiation – for example, after a nuclear explosion. Other leukemias may occur following exposure to industrial chemicals, and a few may be the result of a virus infection. However, in many cases, the cause is unknown.

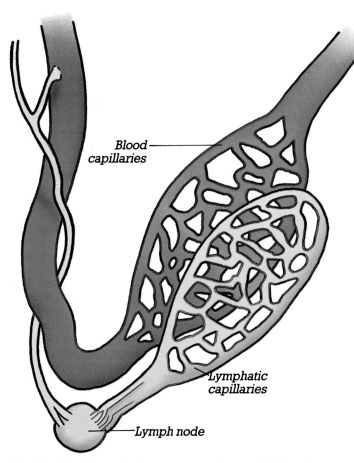

The blood and lymphatic systems exchange fluids and cells. So cancers of the blood often affect the lymphatic system too.

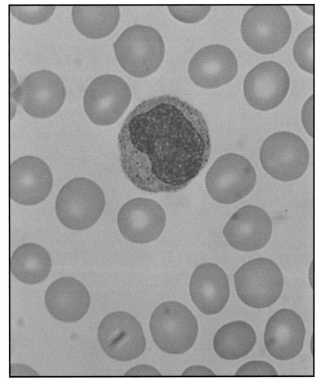

The healthy blood in this microscope picture is rich in red blood cells. The large cell is a white blood cell.

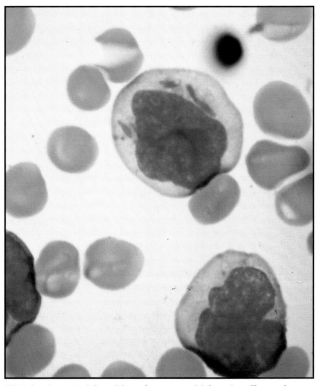

This leukemic blood has fewer red blood cells and a large number of misshapen white blood cells.

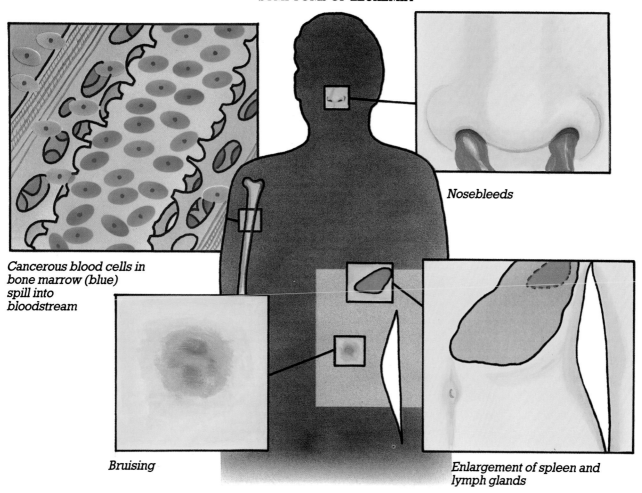

Cancerous blood cells in bone marrow (blue) spill into bloodstream

Nosebleeds

Bruising

Enlargement of spleen and lymph glands

Leukemias tend to destroy the normal workings of blood cells, so the symptoms are nearly all related to problems with the blood and circulation. Patients may feel tired and short of breath because there are not enough red cells in the blood to carry oxygen. There may be bruising on the skin or bleeding from the gums because the blood does not clot properly. (However, there are other causes of these symptoms which have nothing to do with cancer.) The person may suffer from more infections because the abnormal white cells lose their ability to fight infections. Another symptom is swelling. Leukemic cells set up metastases in lymph glands which cause these organs to get bigger.

Some of the white cells in the blood, called lymphocytes, are made in lymph glands. Cancers that develop in these glands are called lymphomas, or lymph cancer. They often cause swelling in the lymph glands, as in Hodgkin's disease. The patient often develops fevers, and becomes quite ill.

HODGKIN'S DISEASE

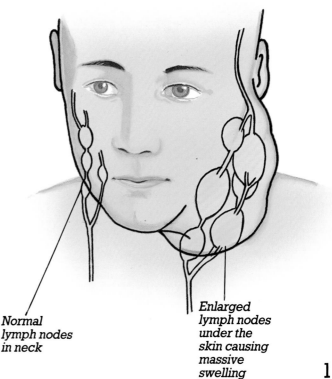

Normal lymph nodes in neck

Enlarged lymph nodes under the skin causing massive swelling

11

The lungs

Most lung cancers are caused by smoking. About one smoker in ten develops lung cancer. The tars in cigarette smoke act as carcinogens and damage the cells which line the fine tubes inside the lungs. When a small tumor has developed in the lungs – perhaps in one of the bronchi or in one of the air sacs, called an alveolus – it tends to spread into the nearby lung tissue.

Some people who develop lung cancer are not smokers. Their cancers may be caused by inhaling other people's cigarette smoke, by air pollution, or by inhaling dangerous dusts, such as asbestos dust. A very small number of lung cancers are caused by natural radioactivity in the atmosphere.

The symptoms of lung cancer include a cough that does not go away, or a cough which produces some blood. Some patients have persistent chest infections. There may also be pains in the chest, but this usually occurs only when the cancer spreads to the wall of the chest.

In some countries it is normal for children to smoke – they face the greatest risk of getting lung cancer and of having it spread to other parts of their bodies.

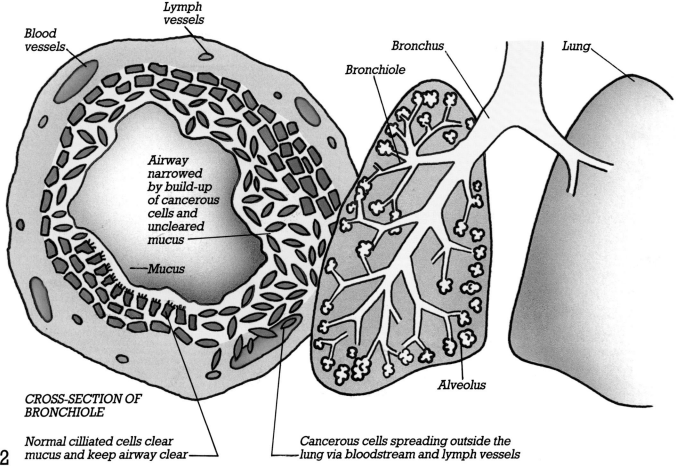

Blood vessels

Lymph vessels

Bronchus

Bronchiole

Lung

Airway narrowed by build-up of cancerous cells and uncleared mucus

Mucus

Alveolus

CROSS-SECTION OF BRONCHIOLE

Normal cilliated cells clear mucus and keep airway clear

Cancerous cells spreading outside the lung via bloodstream and lymph vessels

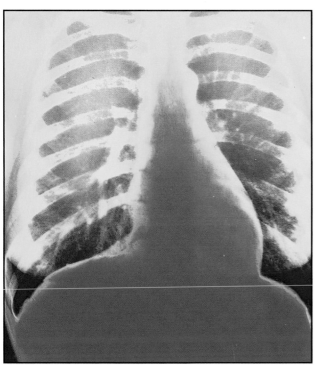

X ray of normal lungs (blue)

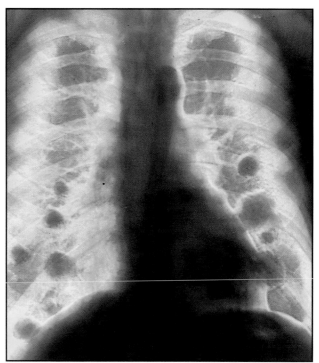

Cancer in both lungs appears as orange shadows.

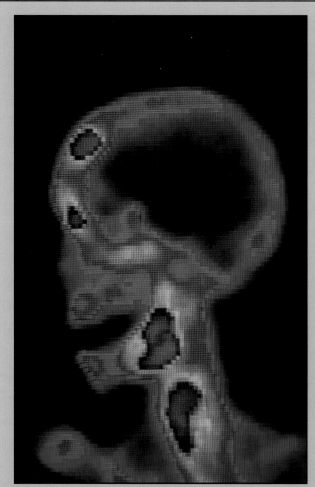

X-ray of skull and neck; red areas show bone cancer.

Bone cancers

Cancer in the bones is quite rare, although it is one of the types of cancer which may affect young adults and sometimes teenagers. The reason for this is that the cancer starts where bone tissue is being made during periods of growth.

All the bones in the body are formed out of a tough, jelly-like substance called cartilage. Gradually, the cartilage is replaced by bone tissue. Bone-forming cells, called osteoblasts, grow into the cartilage and lay down hard, bony tissue. Most bone cancers are the result of a cancerous change which occurs in osteoblasts. A tumor forms, often inside the bone itself.

Cancerous change in bone is often caused by metastasis from cancer elsewhere in the body, such as in the lung. Patients with leukemia often develop some form of bone cancer.

The early symptoms of a bone cancer are usually an abnormal swelling of a bone – often in the leg. There may be some discomfort, but not always. A bone tumor can seriously weaken the bone, which may then fracture quite easily.

13

The digestive system

The digestive system is the passage from the mouth to the anus through which our food passes and is broken down. Cancers of the digestive system (the mouth, esophagus, stomach, small intestine and large intestine) are also common types of cancer, following lung cancer and prostate cancer in men, and breast cancer in women. Most of these cancers affect middle-aged and elderly people.

Diet is a likely cause of many of the different types of cancer which affect the digestive system. Scientists know that certain foods, such as smoked foods, contain chemicals that can act as carcinogens. However, other foods, particularly fruit and vegetables, contain chemicals which actually can protect against cancers. Vitamins, such as Vitamin A and Vitamin C, seem to have a natural ability to increase the body's defenses against carcinogens. People who eat a diet that is low in these substances seem to be more at risk from certain intestinal cancers. Fiber in the diet (found mostly in cereals, nuts, fruit and vegetables) may protect people against cancers of the large intestine.

Drinking too much alcohol over a period can increase the risk of certain cancers, particularly cancer of the liver and of the esophagus.

Cancers in the mouth can cause small tumors on the inside of the lips and on the gums. Chewing tobacco – a habit common in some countries – makes these cancers more likely. A condition called "leukoplakia" (an abnormal white area in the lining of the mouth) may appear first, before a true cancer develops.

Cancer of the stomach may begin as a cancerous tumor in the lining of the stomach, which doctors call a cancerous "polyp," or may, rarely, develop from a stomach ulcer.

Cancer in the colon may also start as a cancerous polyp. A symptom of this is often a change in bowel movements, and there may also be some bleeding from the anus. However, there may be other causes of these symptoms, including conditions such as hemorrhoids, which have nothing to do with cancer.

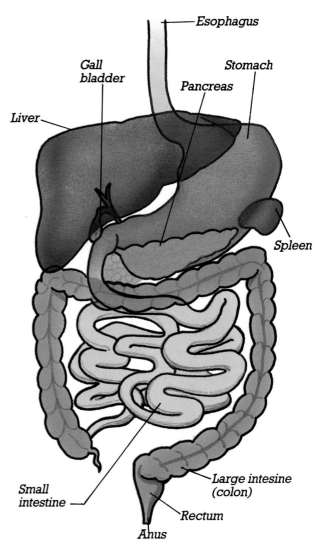

Esophagus

Gall bladder

Stomach

Pancreas

Liver

Spleen

Small intestine

Large intesine (colon)

Rectum

Anus

THE DIGESTIVE SYSTEM

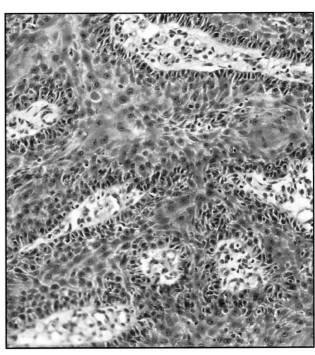

Precancerous conditions of the mouth are fairly common.

14

THE STOMACH

Stomach cancer may start as polyps, which are growths on the stomach lining, or as an ulcer.

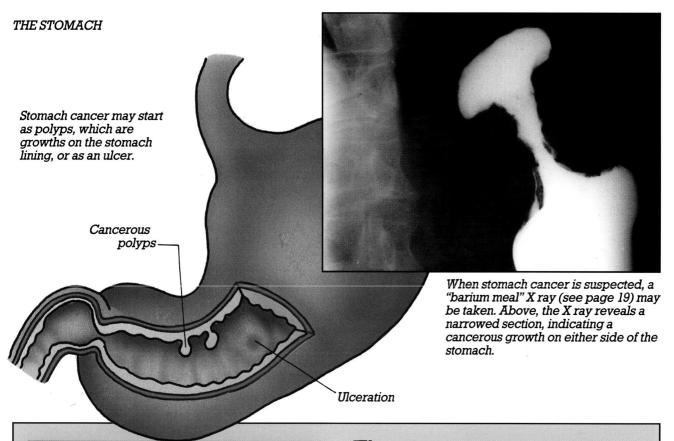

Cancerous polyps

Ulceration

When stomach cancer is suspected, a "barium meal" X ray (see page 19) may be taken. Above, the X ray reveals a narrowed section, indicating a cancerous growth on either side of the stomach.

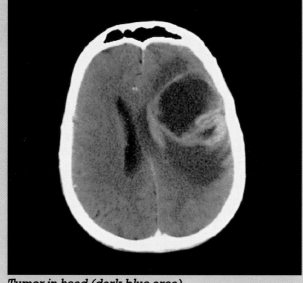

Tumor in head (dark blue area)

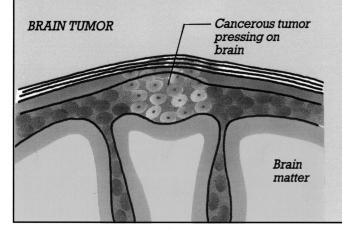

BRAIN TUMOR

Cancerous tumor pressing on brain

Brain matter

The nervous system

Cancers in the nervous system are quite rare, although sometimes metastases from other cancers (such as lung cancer) may occur in the brain.

Cancerous tumors may develop in brain tissue. The tumors expand and cause damage to nearby brain cells. This may result in a person having difficulty with their sight, or with the use of an arm or leg. Sometimes the patient will start having convulsions, or may develop severe headaches. Remember, however, that most headaches are not caused by a brain tumor.

Cancers in other parts of the nervous system are even rarer. Occasionally, a cancer can develop in the spinal cord, which is the main connection between all the nerves of the body and the brain. Depending on its location in the spinal cord, the cancer may cause weakness and numbness in the legs or in the arms. If the cancer is not treated, it may lead to complete paralysis of the affected parts. The spinal cord may also be affected by tumors in the backbone, which can press on the spinal cord as they grow.

15

BREAST CANCER

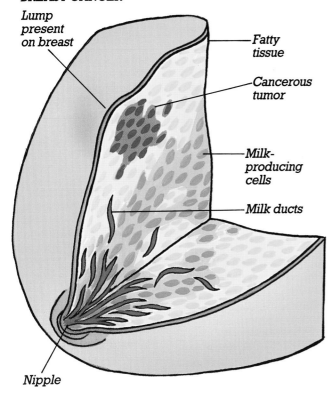

Lump present on breast

Fatty tissue

Cancerous tumor

Milk-producing cells

Milk ducts

Nipple

The female reproductive system

Cancer in the breast is the most common cancer in women. It is still not really certain what causes breast cancer. However, it is more common in women who have a history of breast cancer, who are childless, or have their first child very late in life, or who do not fully breastfeed their babies. Doctors also think that breast cancer may be more common in obese women, but this has not yet been confirmed.

Breast cancer can start at any age in adult life, but it is more common in middle-aged and elderly women. Doctors encourage women to examine their breasts each month for early signs of a cancer. The first sign is often just an unusual lump or swelling in the tissue of the breast. A little fluid may come from the nipple of the breast, stained with blood. There may also be changes to the skin over the lump. However, lumps in the breast are quite common. Many of them are simply cysts or benign tumors, which are mostly harmless. But a woman who discovers a lump in her breast should always go to a doctor so that it can be properly checked.

Breast cancer tends to spread to lymph glands in the armpit, which then grow larger.

Cancers can also develop in the female reproductive organs. The ovaries are the organs which normally produce the eggs (that may be fertilized by sperm from a man to make a baby). Ovaries can be affected by cancer, but this usually occurs in older women. The uterus, which is also called the womb, is the place where a baby grows. The uterus may also be affected by a cancer which starts in the cells that line its walls. These cells are called endometrial cells. Cancers in this part of the uterus tend to develop more often in women who have not had children. Another type of cancer occurs in the cervix, which is the lowest part of the uterus. This area can be examined by a doctor, and regular tests, known as cervical, or Pap, smears, can be done to detect precancer changes in the cells of the cervix.

Cancer of the vagina can also occur, but this tends to be quite rare.

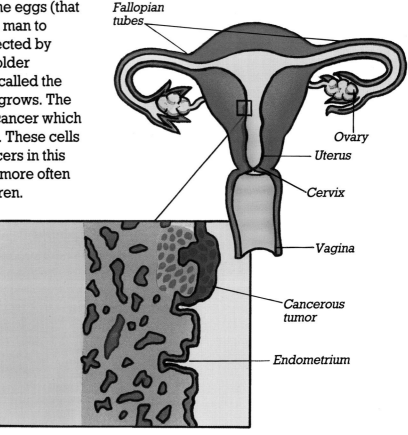

Fallopian tubes

Ovary

Uterus

Cervix

Vagina

Cancerous tumor

Endometrium

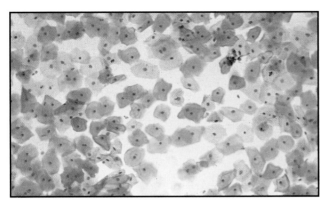

Microscope picture of a Pap smear showing normal uniform cells. Small dots indicate the nucleus of each cell.

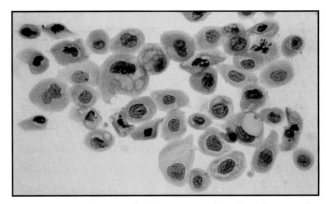

Microscope picture of a Pap smear showing abnormal cells with enlarged nuclei. Pap smears can detect cancer at an early and curable stage.

The male urinary and reproductive systems

Before waste liquid leaves the body as urine, it is stored in the bladder. Cancerous tumors in the bladder do develop in women, but they are more common in men. Sometimes there are many small tumors, called papillomas, but occasionally the tumors may grow to quite a large size and spread to nearby organs. The most common symptom of bladder cancer is blood in the urine (although this sympton may also occur as a result of infections).

The prostate gland is a small gland about the size of a plum and is just below the bladder in a man. The gland makes some of the fluid for semen, that is, the male sexual fluid. Cancers in the prostate gland tend to develop in elderly men. They may grow very slowly, but occasionally they form metastases in other parts of the body. If a cancer develops in the prostate, it tends to block the flow of urine from the bladder.

The testicles are the two round organs inside a bag of skin below the penis. They produce sperm (which may fertilize a female's egg and make a baby). Cancerous tumors can develop in the testicles at any time in adult life, but they are uncommon. Usually they just cause an unusual swelling of a testicle.

Since cancers of the testicle can be cured if they are detected early, it is wise for all men to check their testicles every few weeks to ensure there are no unusual lumps or swelling.

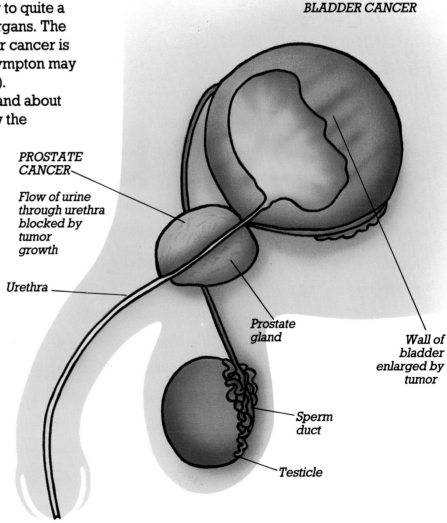

BLADDER CANCER

PROSTATE CANCER

Flow of urine through urethra blocked by tumor growth

Urethra

Prostate gland

Wall of bladder enlarged by tumor

Sperm duct

Testicle

17

TESTS AND DIAGNOSIS

At any consultation with a patient, the doctor usually has quite a good idea of what might be wrong simply as a result of talking with the patient. There are some symptoms which tend to suggest a cancer, such as coughing up blood or a sore that does not heal. Doctors are always on the lookout for such symptoms so it is important that patients describe their symptoms carefully. It may be that the symptoms have a simple explanation and are not caused by a cancer, but the doctor will want to examine the patient carefully and carry out tests to make a firm diagnosis. The earlier a cancer is diagnosed, the more likely it is that treatment will be successful. Treatments are now much more successful than they were even a few years ago. In 1949 only about one quarter of all cancer patients could expect to live for five years after the diagnosis. Now, well over one half of all cancer patients live at least five years. Many cancers are 100 percent curable.

Making a diagnosis

After the doctor has talked with the patient about the symptoms, an examination usually follows. The type of examination will depend on where the trouble appears to be. For example, if the patient complains of chest pain or coughing, the doctor will check the patient's chest carefully and listen to the breathing sounds with a stethoscope. If the trouble appears to be with the bowels or with the stomach, the doctor will examine the abdomen, pressing gently on each area in turn. The doctor will try to detect any abnormal lumps in the abdomen, which could be tumors, and will check other organs, such as the liver and spleen. Often the doctor will want to carry out some form of internal examination – for example, a rectal examination – with a special instrument. If the patient is a woman, the doctor may perform a vaginal examination to check the uterus and the ovaries. The breasts may also be examined.

Often, the patient will be asked to provide one or more specimens which are then tested. Blood tests may be needed to see how well various functions of the body are working. Sometimes a simple blood test may help to diagnose leukemia, but it can rarely be used to make a firm diagnosis of other cancers. A urine sample may also be needed for the diagnosis.

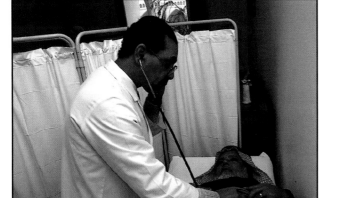

Examination

A mammogram, or breast X ray

18

X ray photographs, taken after a barium meal, of the stomach (above) and the colon. The narrow area in the lower picture indicates a tumor.

Barium X rays

A doctor who suspects a cancer in the esophagus or stomach will want to see an X ray of the patient. However, these parts of the body do not show up well on X rays, so the patient has to have a special kind of X ray called a "barium meal." For this, the patient swallows a thick fluid, containing a chemical – barium sulfate. This chemical coats the esophagus and stomach which will then show up on the X ray picture. The patient lies on a special X ray table which can be tipped in various directions so that the doctor can get a good view of all parts of both the esophagus and the stomach. Stomach ulcers will show up on the X ray, as well as cancerous polyps.

Another kind of X ray is used if a cancer is suspected in the colon, the lower part of the intestine. This is called a barium enema.

Looking inside

Doctors now use special instruments to look inside various parts of the body. These instruments are called endoscopes and usually consist of a long, flexible tube which contains a fiberoptic system. This lights up parts of the body and sends a picture back to the doctor. There is a tiny pair of forceps at the end of the endoscope, so a doctor is also able to take samples of suspicious tissues, which scientists can then analyze in a laboratory. (This kind of sample is called a biopsy.) Bronchoscopes are used to examine the lungs; gastroscopes examine the stomach; cystoscopes examine the bladder; laparoscopes examine the organs in the abdomen and the internal female organs. Usually, the patient is given an anesthetic for these tests.

Using a bronchoscope

19

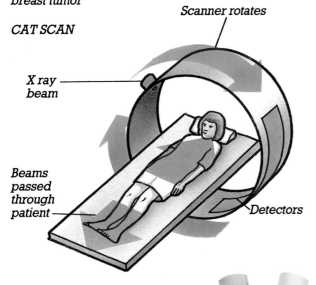

Arteriogram (X ray highlighted with dyes) reveals breast tumor

How X rays help in diagnosis

Cancers are sometimes diagnosed with the help of various different types of X ray. An ordinary X ray shows up bones very well, so bone cancers can often be diagnosed by a simple X ray. Sometimes lung cancers show up on an ordinary chest X ray, too. Often, however, special X ray techniques are needed.

A mammogram is a type of X ray used to detect tumors in the breast. The woman's breast is placed over an X ray plate and held in place with gentle pressure. The X ray picture can show quite small abnormalities in the breast tissue.

A more complicated technique for detecting cancers in some parts of the body is called arteriography. The doctor injects a special dye called a contrast medium directly into blood vessels, and this makes them show up on an X ray. The contrast medium enters through a fine tube which is threaded into the large arteries of the body at the groin. Alternatively, the injection can be carefully positioned so that it shows the circulation of blood in just one area. This method will show up any abnormal blood vessels in tumors. A similar technique can be used to show the internal structure of lymph nodes. In this case, the doctor injects the contrast medium into a lymph vessel in one of the patient's feet.

Another special technique is Computerized Axial Tomography, or a CAT Scan for short. The patient has to lie very still as a fine, pencil-thin X ray beam is passed through the body to a detector lying on the opposite side of the body. The beam and the detectors rotate around the patient's body while a computer builds up a picture of the patient's insides. The resulting picture shows a cross section of one part of the body. This technique is valuable for diagnosing brain tumors.

CAT SCAN

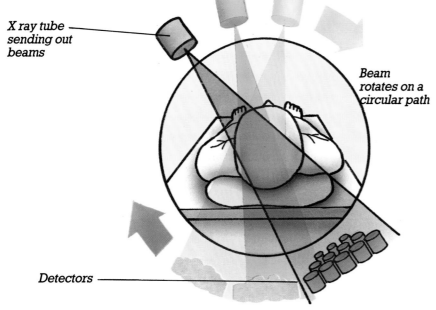

Scanner rotates

X ray beam

Beams passed through patient

Detectors

X ray tube sending out beams

Beam rotates on a circular path

Detectors

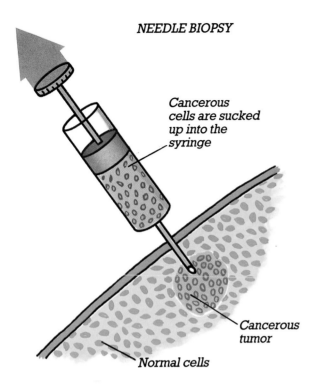

NEEDLE BIOPSY

Cancerous cells are sucked up into the syringe

Cancerous tumor

Normal cells

Biopsy

X rays and blood tests will give the doctor a good idea of the nature of the patient's problem. However, a final diagnosis of cancer usually depends on an examination of a small piece of the tumor in a laboratory. Specialist doctors called pathologists can then tell exactly what sort of tumor it is and whether it is benign or cancerous. The removal of a piece of tumor for examination is called a biopsy. In the case of a skin tumor, the biopsy can be carried out easily under local or general anesthetic. Sometimes a doctor will use an endoscope to carry out a biopsy of internal organs. At other times a needle may be inserted into a tumor and its cells sucked up into a syringe for examination. This method is quite easy to use, although not always suitable, and is called a needle biopsy.

Surgery

Once a diagnosis of cancer has been made, the doctor arranges for suitable treatment. In many cases, this will involve surgery. Many skin cancers are usually removed completely by surgery under local anesthetic without much difficulty.

Cancers in deeper organs in the body usually need more complicated surgery. Sometimes lung cancer can be removed by surgery. Part of the lung, or even a whole lung with the cancer still inside it may be removed. Stomach or intestinal cancers can also sometimes be removed by surgery.

Cancer in the uterus may be treated by the removal of the uterus, an operation which is called hysterectomy. Breast cancers can be treated by removal of the cancerous lump (a lumpectomy). However, often the surgeon may advise that the whole breast be removed. This operation is called mastectomy.

When cancer surgery is performed, the surgeon sometimes tries to remove all the nearby lymph glands. It is possible that the cancer may have spread to these glands. By removing the lymph glands, the surgeon will be trying to remove possible metastases and so prevent further spread of the cancer.

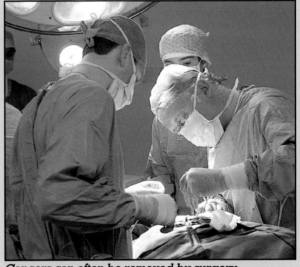

Cancers can often be removed by surgery.

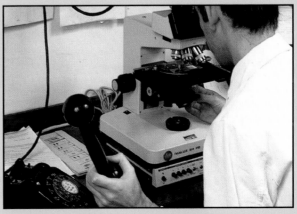

Lumps are analyzed under a microscope.

21

Radiotherapy

Many years ago scientists found that cancer cells in the body can be damaged quite easily by high doses of X rays. Although normal body cells may also be damaged to some extent by X rays, they tend to heal afterward, whereas cancer cells die off. Radiotherapy treatment for cancer aims to kill cancer cells deep inside the body. Special machines beam X rays very accurately onto the patient's body so that the highest dose of X rays is given to the area where the tumor is located. Gamma rays are also used for radiotherapy. Often several treatments are given over a period of days or weeks.

Radiotherapy is also given by implanting needles, tubes, wires or tiny particles of a radioactive substance into a tumor.

Radiotherapy may be used as the only treatment for certain types of cancer. It can be used in addition to surgery. The patient may first have an operation to remove the main cancer and then radiation treatments to kill any cancer cells that remain.

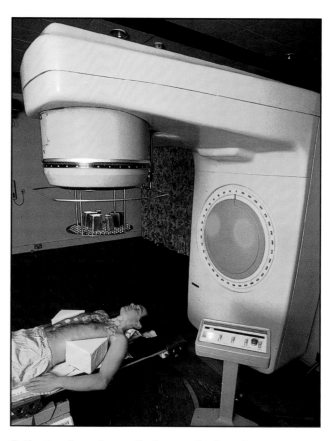

Patient undergoing radiotherapy for lymph cancer. Areas to be treated appear as illuminated circles.

Chemotherapy

A number of different drugs can be used to treat cancers. Any treatment of this kind is called chemotherapy. Doctors may give the drugs as pills or tablets, but often they either inject them or give them by a drip straight into the patient's bloodstream. Many of the drugs which are used are very poisonous and damage normal body cells. However, as with radiotherapy, cancer cells are affected much more by these drugs than ordinary body cells. They tend to die, whereas normal body tissues can recover.

Often, many different drugs are used at the same time – perhaps four or six different types at once. Chemotherapy is used as the only treatment for many types of leukemia or lymph cancers. It is also used for other cancers in combination with surgery, or with radiotherapy.

Sometimes drugs are given to treat cancer that affect hormone levels in the body. They work in a different way from other types of chemotherapy. They may, for example, be given as treatment for breast cancer.

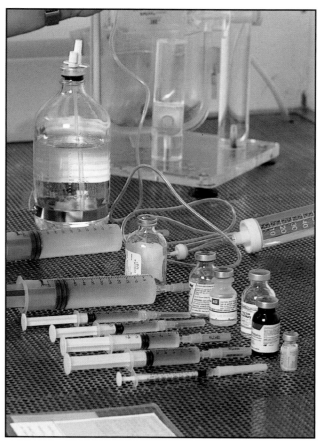

Chemotherapy often involves the use of several different drugs; some taken as tablets, others injected.

Problems

Radiotherapy and chemotherapy often cause side effects. Both types of treatment can make the patient feel sick for a time. Radiotherapy may sometimes make the skin sore. Chemotherapy often makes people lose their hair and be nauseated. But side effects usually pass and, as the treatment begins to work, the patient starts to feel better.

Radiotherapy and chemotherapy can reduce the number of white cells in the bloodstream. Shortly after treatment, the patient may be at extra risk from infections because there are not enough white cells in the blood to fight them off. Transfusions of white cells may be needed at this point. This particular side effect is now used deliberately in the treatment of certain types of leukemias. Doctors will give drugs and radiotherapy to these patients in order to kill off the bone marrow completely – together with all the leukemic cells. The patient is then given new bone marrow cells from another person – a bone marrow donor. These cells act as a transplant, and replace the bone marrow, which starts to work normally again.

Chemotherapy can cause hair loss.

Cells from bone marrow donor syringed out

Bone marrow

COURSE OF CHEMOTHERAPY

Blood count X10

Start treatment

End treatment

2

1

Days of treatment   7   14   21

High risk of infection

Bone marrow is frozen until required for transplant.

LIVING WITH CANCER

It is often difficult for people to come to terms with the fact that they have been diagnosed as having a cancer. Yet, often the treatment will bring about a complete cure, or at least allow many years of happy life. Treatment may keep the cancer under control so that the person has no symptoms, even if the cancerous tumor is still present.

It is very important for the person to be aware of what is happening and to know what to expect from the treatment. Although some treatments have side effects, these are usually temporary, and it is easier to cope with side effects if one knows what to expect. Some years ago, many doctors did not tell their patients when they had diagnosed a cancer in order to avoid upsetting them. Today, most doctors believe that it is very important that patients should know what is wrong. Doctors usually discuss the results of tests quite openly with their patients and help them gradually to come to terms with the diagnosis.

Staying in the hospital

The hospital can be frightening. To normally healthy people, they are unfamiliar places, with strange smells and strange sights. While doctors and nurses rush about, many patients feel alienated and anxious, and have little idea of what to expect. This is especially true when a patient is already frightened about his or her illness.

It need not feel so frightening. It is important for anybody going into the hospital to know what is likely to happen to them, and to feel that he or she has some control over their own case. So, patients should always ask plenty of questions. First, they should ask their own doctor why it is that they need to go into the hospital in the first place, and what tests are likely to be done. Once in the hospital, patients should make sure that nurses and doctors tell them what is happening at every stage. Anyone who is to have treatment should know first what kind of treatment it is, why it is being given and what possible side effects there might be. The same applies to any operation that is planned. In addition, if there is a possibility that the patient may need to go to an intensive care ward after an operation, then this should be explained to him or her well in advance. Otherwise waking up from the anesthetic could be a frightening experience.

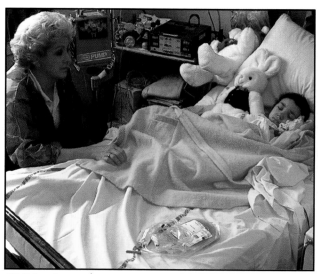
Children's ward

Child in sterilized tent

24

Positive thinking

Recent research has shown that people who have a very positive, happy attitude about themselves and their lives are likely to recover better after treatment for cancer than those people who give up and feel helpless. One reason for this is that the body's immune system can attack and destroy cancer cells best when the patient is free from stress. People with positive attitudes also feel less pain and discomfort.

Anyone who has had treatment for cancer should have plenty of rest and relaxation, but they should also start making some plans for the future. The plans may just involve the next day, or the day after, or weeks ahead. The important point is that the person must be encouraged to live for the future, rather than just living from day to day.

White blood cells of the body's immune system attacking a cancer cell

The control of symptoms

Despite the many successes of cancer treatment, some cancers cannot be cured completely. The patient may be left with some symptoms – a feeling of sickness, shortage of breath or pain. Some patients may lose weight. However, in many cases, the patient can be helped to feel better with the right kind of medical treatment. For example, there are several different kinds of treatment that can relieve nausea. There are many different types of pain-killing drugs. Special hospitals called hospices have opened in some areas and home care programs are increasing. Hospices are run by doctors and nurses who aim to relieve the patients' symptoms and make them feel comfortable and happy again.

Hospices also try to help patients feel more at ease with themselves and with their families. Although it is upsetting for friends and relatives to know that someone they love may not have very long to live, their support and love is vital. ·

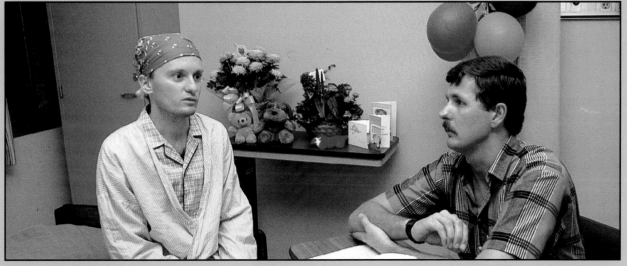

Hospice for the terminally ill

Screening

In many cases, routine examinations and tests will detect cancers when they are at a very early stage. Any cancer that is found can be treated while the tumor is still very small. Screening programs aim to check everybody who may be at risk from a particular cancer.

Breast cancer: The simplest screening procedure is for all women to examine their own breasts carefully every month to check for the presence of any unusual lumps.

Cervical cancer: Precancerous changes in the cells of the cervix can be easily detected through a cervical smear test, or Pap test. These changes can be easily treated. In fact, recent studies indicate that regular Pap tests can reduce the death rate from cervical cancer by 75%.

Cancer of the testicle: Doctors now suggest that all men check their testicles every month, looking for lumps, swelling or hardness, which could be tumors.

Other cancers: Workers in certain industries who are at risk from occupational cancers should be screened. For example, workers in the asbestos industry should be screened for lung changes that may indicate the early stages of cancer.

CERVICAL SMEAR

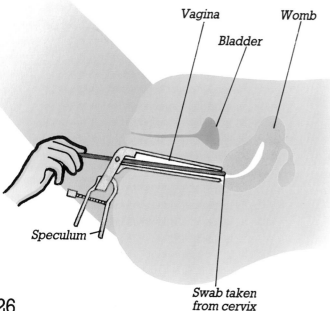

Vagina

Womb

Bladder

Speculum

Swab taken
from cervix

BREAST EXAMINATION

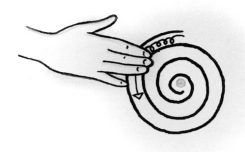

Feel with the flats of the fingers in circular movements covering the entire breast

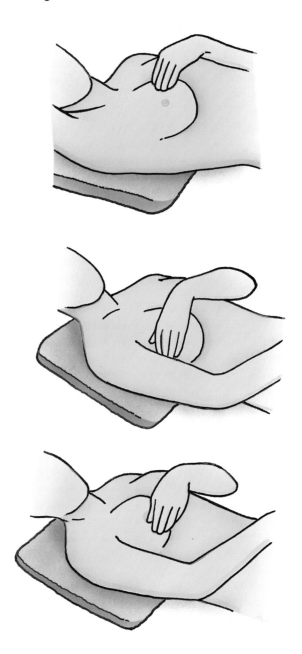

Hopes for the future

Vast amounts of money are spent every year on research to try to reduce the problem of cancer. There are several different types of research being carried out.

First, researchers are trying to find out more about the causes of cancer. If we knew more about the causes, then it might be possible to prevent more cancers. Some of the best known research of this type has been into the effects of cigarette smoke. Some years ago it was discovered that most patients with lung cancer had been smokers at some time in their lives. People who had never smoked were much less likely to have lung cancer. In time, the specific substances in cigarette smoke which cause the cancer were found. More recent research has concentrated on radiation and the role of diet in causing cancers. Some researchers are trying to find out more about why some people develop cancers after exposure to a carcinogen while other people remain unaffected.

The second main area of research is into better ways of detecting cancers early. It is possible that a simple blood test might eventually be able to pinpoint people who have early cancer. The test could then be carried out routinely on everyone.

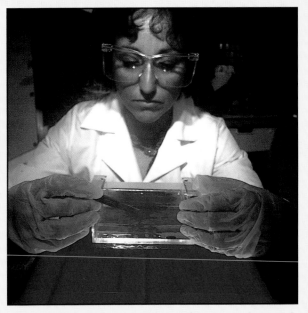

Research labs are constantly working to understand and find a cure for cancer.

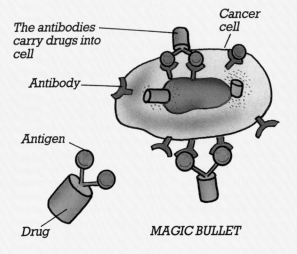

The antibodies carry drugs into cell

Cancer cell

Antibody

Antigen

Drug

MAGIC BULLET

LASER SURGERY A fine tube is inserted through the body to the tumor using ultrasound scanners

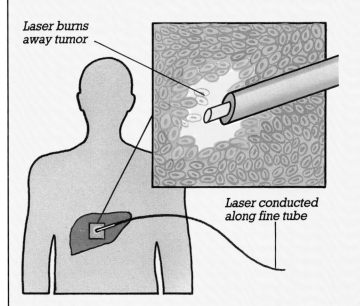

Laser burns away tumor

Laser conducted along fine tube

Lastly, there is a great deal of research into new methods of treatment. For example, new surgical techniques are always being developed. Surgeons now use a laser beam in some cases to remove very small areas of cancerous or precancerous tissue. New drugs are always being developed. One hope for the future is a magic bullet treatment. Scientists use this name to describe a drug that homes in on cancer cells to destroy them, while leaving normal cells untouched. However, like many possible miracle cures, progress is slow and it may be some years before this type of treatment is available.

27

TAKING CARE OF YOUR BODY

We already know enough about the causes of cancer to be able to prevent at least one half of all cancers and possibly even more. Almost everyone can reduce their risks of developing cancer by following a few simple guidelines. We need to have respect for our bodies and avoid exposing ourselves to substances which could cause damage.

The responsibility for preventing cancer does not just lie with the individual. Employers must make sure that there are no risks at work. If carcinogenic chemicals are used in a factory, there must be proper safety precautions. Governments also have a responsibility. They must ensure that the health services provide proper screening programs, and that quick treatment is available for anyone who does have a cancer. Governments must make sure that the food supply is safe and that it is not contaminated with chemicals which could be carcinogenic.

Diet and healthy living

The importance of a good diet in preventing cancer has become much clearer over the past few years. Researchers have found high cancer rates in some countries that are associated with particular types of diet. When people move from one part of the world to another and then change their diets, their risk of developing some cancers can also change. However, if they keep to their original diet, the cancer risk stays the same. It is possible for scientists to determine whether or not people have a high or low risk of certain cancers as a result of eating particular types of food. From research of this type it has been found that diets which are high in fat tend to be associated with some types of bowel cancer, and that being overweight also increases the risk of cancer. Drinking too much alcohol may cause cancers in the mouth, the throat, the esophagus and the liver.

The advice on diet is:
* Eat plenty of fruit and vegetables, particularly green, leafy vegetables and yellow and orange fruit and vegetables.
* Cut down on fatty foods. Choose lean meat or fish. Keep butter and cheese to a minimum and drink a low-fat milk.
* Avoid being overweight.
* Adults should follow the recommended guidelines on alcohol.

Different diets cause different digestive problems.

Many cancer patients are completely cured after their treatment.

28

Prevention

Smoking: The most important preventive measure that anyone can take to avoid cancer is not to smoke. Smokers are 40 times more likely to get lung cancer than nonsmokers; they are also more likely to develop cancers in the throat and the bladder. Nearly one third of all cancers are caused by smoking.

Children and young people should not start smoking. Parents and teachers have a duty to try to make sure that children understand the dangers of smoking, which also causes heart disease and chronic bronchitis. It is vital for the health of established smokers that they should give it up. This may prove very difficult. Smokers must convince themselves of how important it is for their health that they stop, and can ask their colleagues at work, their family and friends to help them. If necessary, the family doctor may be able to help with advice, and there are numerous support groups available for those trying to kick the habit.

The good news is that once a smoker stops smoking, the risks of developing cancer and other diseases begin to decrease almost immediately.

The sun: Too much sun causes skin cancer. If you have fair skin, you should be especially careful. Always use plenty of sunscreen and tan very slowly. At all costs, avoid getting burned by the sun.

At work: Obey health and safety rules. The handling of many substances (such as asbestos) is controlled by law.

Screening: All women should have breast and Pap screening. Everyone should have a regular dental checkup.

The high risk of asbestos means total protection is needed.

Advice to smokers: quit now.
*Advice to nonsmokers: never, **ever** start.*

Protection from the sun in the form of sunscreen creams will reduce the risk of skin cancer.

Seven warning signs

Any of the seven signs listed below may be due to a minor illness, but sometimes there is a more serious cause. It is important for anyone with one or more of these signs to see a doctor for a checkup. Tests may then be needed to discover whether a cancer is a possible cause.

1 Any change in the way the bowels work (for example, if you have diarrhea or are constipated), if this change lasts for more than a week.

2 A sore throat, a hoarse voice or a nagging cough that lasts for more than a week.

3 Bleeding from an unusual place (for example, blood in the urine when you go to the bathroom).

4 Lumps appearing under the skin (for example, in a woman's breast or on a man's testicles).

5 Indigestion that lasts for longer than a few days.

6 Pain on swallowing food.

7 A mole on the skin which bleeds or starts to grow bigger.

Useful addresses

American Cancer Society
1599 Clifton Road, N.E.
Atlanta, Georgia 30329
(404) 320-3333

American Society of Pediatric Hemotology/Oncology
Michael Reese Hospital
Dept. of Pediatrics
2915 S. Ellis
Chicago, Illinois 60616
(312) 791-4206

Cancer Assistance League International
18 Bayou Shadows
Houston, Texas 77024
(713) 461-5100

Cancer Care Counseling Line at UCLA
Jonsson Comprehensive Cancer Center
10920 Wiltshire Boulevard
Suite 1106
Los Angeles, California 90024
(213) 206-6017

Cancer Care, Inc.
1180 Avenue of the Americas
New York, New York 10036
(212) 221-3300

Cancer Lifeline
500 Lowman Building
107 Cherry Street
Seattle, Washington 98104
(206) 447 4542

Cancer Support Network
802 E. Jefferson
Bloomington, Illinois 61701
(309) 829-2273

Lukemia Society of America, Inc.
733 Third Avenue
New York, New York 10017
(212) 573-8484

Office of Cancer Communication National Cancer Institute
National Institute of Health
Bethesda, Maryland 20014
1 (800) 4-CANCER

Glossary

Antibody A substance that is produced in the body and that fights against an antigen.

Antigen A potentially harmful substance that causes the body to make an antibody.

Benign The name doctors use to describe a growth in the body that is not cancerous and does not spread to other tissues.

Carcinogen A chemical that affects the internal structure of a cell, turning it into a cancer cell.

Cervix The neck, or lower part, of the uterus (womb).

Colon The large intestine.

Cyst A growth in the body which is hollow and contains liquid.

DNA The chemicals that make up the genetic material of body cells. DNA controls all the functions of a cell.

Hormone A chemical that is made in the body by an endocrine gland, circulates in the bloodstream and controls the actions of another part of the body.

Hysterectomy An operation to remove the uterus (womb) from a woman.

Inflammation A sore swelling.

Laser A special form of high-intensity light.

Leukemia The name that doctors give to all cancers of the blood cells and the bone marrow.

Lymph system A system of very fine vessels which run through all the tissues of the body. A watery fluid called lymph drains through these vessels into lymph glands. Lymph glands helps to remove and destroy bacteria.

Lymphoma A cancer of the lymph system.

Malignant The name doctors use to describe a growth in the body that is cancerous and may spread to other tissues.

Mastectomy An operation to remove a breast from a woman.

Melanoma A cancer of pigment cells in the skin.

Metastasis (plural: Metastases) A cancerous growth that develops as a result of cancer cells spreading from one area of the body to another, often through the bloodstream or the lymph system.

Organ A group of tissues in the body that work together to perform a certain function or number of functions, for example the heart is an organ that pumps blood.

Pathologist A doctor who specializes in carrying out tests on samples of blood, on other body fluids and on samples of tissues. These tests help to make a diagnosis in suspected cases of cancer.

Spleen An organ, about the size of a fist, which is under the ribs on the left-hand side. It works as part of the lymph system.

Stethoscope An instrument used by a doctor to listen to sounds from inside the body.

Symptoms Anything a patient may feel in the body or the mind that is caused by disease or illness.

Tissue A group of cells in the body that are of the same type, for example muscle cells.

Tumor A disorganized growth of cells in the body where cells should not be growing.

Virus A tiny microbe that can cause disease.

INDEX

Photographic Credits:
Cover and page 23 top, 28 bottom and 29 top: Frank Spooner Agency; pages 5, 9 top, 10 left and right, 13 left and right, 14, 15, top and bottom, 17 left and right, 18 bottom, 19 top and bottom, 20, 21 top, 22 top and bottom, 23 bottom, 24 top and bottom, 25 top, 27 top and 29 left: Science Photo Library; pages 9 bottom, 12, 18 top, 28 top and 29 right: Robert Harding Library; page 19 middle: Biophoto Associates; page 21 bottom: National Medical Slide Bank; page 25 bottom: Rex Features.